AR BL 1.7 pts 0.5 Quiz 135941

DATE DUE

		FEB 2 8 2011
MAY 1 6 2011		
SEP 1 0 2010		
	FEB 1 4 2011	FEB 2 8 2011
SEP 2 0 2010	APR 1 3 2011	
SEP 2 9 2010	MAY 0 8 2011	
SEP 2 7 2010		
	NOV 1 6 2011	
OCT 2 7 2010	JAN 1 3 2012	
NOV 0 3 2010		
NOV 1 6 2010		
DEC 1 3 2010	JAN 1 7 2012	
JAN 1 4 2011		
MAR 1 1 2011		
MAR 1 5 2010	MAY 2 0 2011	
MAR 2 8 2011		
MAR 2 4 2011		
MAY 0 2 2011		
OCT 1 9 2011		

DEMCO 38-296

Meet the LION

Susanna Keller

PowerKiDS press.
New York

Published in 2010 by The Rosen Publishing Group, Inc.
29 East 21st Street, New York, NY 10010

First Edition

Editor: Amelie von Zumbusch
Book Design: Kate Laczynski
Photo Researcher: Jessica Gerweck

Photo Credits: Cover, pp. 1, 4, 6, 10, 12, 14, 16, 18, 20, 22 Shutterstock.com; p. 8 Getty Images/Holly Harris.

Library of Congress Cataloging-in-Publication Data

Keller, Susanna.
  Meet the lion / Susanna Keller. — 1st ed.
      p. cm. — (At the zoo)
  Includes index.
  ISBN 978-1-4358-9309-2 (library binding) — ISBN 978-1-4358-9730-4 (pbk.) — ISBN 978-1-4358-9731-1 (6 pack)
  1. Lions—Juvenile literature. I. Title.
  QL737.C23K456 2010
  599.757—dc22

                                        2009018898

Manufactured in the United States of America

CPSIA Compliance Information: Batch #WW10PK: For Further Information contact Rosen Publishing, New York, New York at 1-800-237-9932

CONTENTS

Have you ever seen a lion?
Lions are big, powerful cats.

Lions have strong **paws** and sharp teeth. They are excellent hunters.

Lions can be a danger to people. The safest way to see a lion is to visit one in a zoo.

9

10

These big cats eat meat. Zoos supply lions with plenty of meat.

Zoos also make sure that lions have enough water to drink.

14

Lions most often live in groups. A group of lions is called a **pride**.

Most prides have one or two males. Male lions have **manes**.

Female lions do not have manes. In the wild, the female lions do most of a pride's hunting.

Female lions are good mothers. Their babies are known as **cubs**.

22

Lion cubs are playful. The cubs want to find out everything about the world around them.

WORDS TO KNOW

cub

mane

paw

pride

INDEX

WEB SITES

Due to the changing nature of Internet links, PowerKids Press has developed an online list of Web sites related to the subject of this book. This site is updated regularly. Please use this link to access the list:
www.powerkidslinks.com/atzoo/lion/